THE SOLITARY THRONE

Photo: Abraham, Keswick

Dr. SAMUEL M. ZWEMER

THE
SOLITARY THRONE

ADDRESSES GIVEN AT THE
KESWICK CONVENTION
ON THE GLORY AND
THE UNIQUENESS OF
THE CHRISTIAN MESSAGE

BY

Dr. S. M. ZWEMER

Professor of Christian Missions and the History
of Religion, Princeton Theological Seminary

WIPF & STOCK · Eugene, Oregon

Wipf and Stock Publishers
199 W 8th Ave, Suite 3
Eugene, OR 97401

The Solitary Throne
Addresses Given at the Keswick Convention on
the Glory and the Uniqueness of the Christian Message
By Zwemer, Samuel M.
ISBN 13: 978-1-62032-033-4
Publication date 3/1/2012
Previously published by Pickering & Inglis, 1938

Preface

THIS little book consists of five addresses given at the Keswick Convention in the summer of 1937. The title is borrowed from a statement made by Mahatma Gandhi in one of his books: " I am unable to place Jesus Christ on a solitary throne." He believes, as do all Hindus, in many incarnations, and not in the unique origin, character and messages of our Saviour. The finality of Christianity is being challenged even in so-called Christian circles. But the Lamb is on the Throne and He alone is worthy to open the seals of the Book of Life and History.

The other addresses deal with the same theme of the matchless Christ, Who makes His ministers a flame of fire, and Who Himself dwells in light inaccessible and full of glory. And in Whose light is the life of men.

PREFACE

The last chapter shows how feeble is our faith in view of the greatness of God's promises, and the wealth of our heritage. May the messages in this printed form be used of God, more widely than they were when first uttered.

SAMUEL M. ZWEMER.

EDINBURGH, *August, 1937*.

Contents

		PAGE
I.	THE SOLITARY THRONE,	9
II.	HIS MINISTERS A FLAME,	31
III.	PHOTOPHOBIA,	55
IV.	THE GLORY OF THE IMPOSSIBLE,	77
V.	THE HINTERLAND OF THE SOUL,	95

I

The Solitary Throne

UNLESS Jesus Christ is Lord of all He is not Lord at all. It has often impressed me as a great and very solemn truth that on two of the most solemn occasions in the life of our Lord upon earth, His self-assertion and the utter audacity of His claims were such as to prevent His classification with men. The self-assertion and utter audacity of His claims on these occasions make it impossible for anyone who reads the Gospels to doubt that Jesus Christ is Lord of all.

Both of these occasions were almost parentheses. They were when Christ was in the synagogue at Capernaum, when He burst into a thanksgiving to His Father, using these words: "I thank Thee, O Father, Lord of Heaven and earth, because Thou hast hid these things from the wise and prudent and hast revealed them unto babes. For so it seemed good in Thy sight."

The other occasion was an interruption. Madame Guyon says that "the interruptions are the opportunities." That is a great statement, because if you will take the interruptions in the work of Jesus, or in the words of Jesus, you will find that every interruption was the revelation of a new splendour in the character of our Lord.

Here a question was asked by Thomas: " How can we know the way? " " Jesus saith unto him, I am the Way, the Truth, and the Life; no man cometh unto the Father, but by Me."

No person with ordinary intelligence who reads even these two passages in the Gospels of Matthew and John, can doubt for a moment that, whatever the world may say, Christ asserted His absoluteness and finality. He said that He was the only channel of truth and life and light. The aloofness and the transcendence of Jesus, the Son of Man, are so self-evident, that anyone who accepts the New Testament can only come to that conclusion as to the face value of Christ in His own Book.

It is so easy for us at home here to sing: " All hail the power of Jesu's Name! " But, all round the world, rival faiths and new religions and strange cults are challenging this hymn of the Church which ascribes all glory and praise and honour

THE SOLITARY THRONE 11

to Jesus Christ our Lord. And therefore it is hard to be a witnessing Christian. How hard it is to be a Christian witnessing for Christ over against the testimony of other voices that challenge Christ's supremacy, or that supplant Him in the hearts and lives of men and women and little children.

At home and abroad, even in Christian circles, there are many voices that are raised against the supremacy and the finality and the sufficiency of the Christian religion. Many people who profess and call themselves Christians have lost the sense of Christ's supremacy and sufficiency, and therefore also the urgency of their message.

And there is confusion of tongues, as we all know. When a Methodist bishop in America asserts in public that Mahatma Gandhi is the greatest Christian in India, one begins to wonder what it means when Gandhi says in his latest book : " I cannot place Christ on a solitary throne, because I believe God has been incarnate again and again." Or when in the Student Movement of America, one of our former leaders uses in his book, " Christ or Christianity ? " words like these : " One of the most tragic blunders of Christendom has been the placing of such extreme emphasis upon the uniqueness of Jesus that an unbridgeable gulf has been created between Him and the rest of mankind. If all human beings were created in the spiritual image of God, and if there is only one kind of personality, then the only difference between Jesus and other men is one of maturity."

Wilhelm Hauer, a representative of the neo-paganism of Germany, and a Professor in one of the Universities there, uses words like these : " The Ten Commandments laid down in the Scriptures do not suffice for the building up of the present-day Christianity. The Semitic character of Christianity is undoubted, but such is also its condemnation. Jesus said : 'Salvation is of the Jews,' but He was mistaken. Belief in the Resurrection is not the heart of Christianity, but is a worldly doctrine. Many of Jesus' words and deeds touch a chord deep in our hearts. But we protest against His being imposed on us as a leader and pattern. We must not allow our native religious life, which grows immediately out of our own genius, to be diverted into any Semitic foreign tracks."

Voices like these appear to you and me as being unusual. But I submit that the

THE SOLITARY THRONE 13

great non-Christian religions to-day, that every Mohammedan mosque built in London or Berlin or Paris or New York, every temple to Christian Science, is a direct challenge to the supremacy and the finality of Jesus Christ. In what sense is Christ different from all other religious leaders and personalities? What is His pre-eminence?

When we look at Him we see that the historic Jesus rises, like an inaccessible peak of the Himalayas, above all other mountains and foothills of human greatness. Man's effort has failed to measure His height. History, philosophy, art, have already paid Him their highest tribute. Every newspaper published in New York, in Chicago, in Buenos Ayres, in London, has on its front page an acknowledgment of the Christ of history. It is 1937, A.D.

He is the historic dividing line between what happened before He came, and what happened after His revelation. Even Mohammed in Arabia, as a keen student once said, had Christ on the brain. He could not leave Jesus Christ alone. And in the Koran he speaks of Him as " The Spirit of God, the Word of Truth."

Napoleon on St. Helena said: " I know men, and Jesus was no man. Charlemagne, Alexander the Great, and I, founded great empires upon force, and here is One who founded an empire upon love. And now I am alone and forsaken, and there are millions who would die for Him."

Jean Paul Richter, of Germany, in a wonderful passage, said: " O Thou who art mightiest among the mighty, and the holiest among the holy, Thou with Thy pierced hands, hast lifted empires off their hinges, and turned the tide of human history!"

Rabbi Klausner, the President of the University in Jerusalem, in one of his books on Jesus Christ, says: " His parables are matchless; His ethics are unsurpassed by anything in the Old Testament; He is the supreme fruit of the tree of Judaism."

Now all that is very beautiful, but it is in a sense inadequate, and beside the point. Who is this Jesus Christ Who said that if He were lifted up He would draw all men unto Him? In what respect is Jesus Christ on *a solitary throne?* In what respect is Jesus Christ the Alpha and Omega, the first and the last, the beginning and the end of all human thought, and all human ideals in religion?

Surely missionaries ought not to be narrow-minded; and all of us, I think, who have been abroad, and have had opportunity to study the faiths of non-Christians, are quite willing to admit that these religions which are nearly all older than Christianity have much to commend them. They have certain spiritual and moral values.

In Confucianism you have the sacredness of the family. No Chinese boy would ever speak to his father as some American lads do. In Hinduism you have the great conception of the immanence of God:

> "Speak to Him, thou, for He hears,
>   And Spirit with spirit can meet.
> Closer is He than breathing,
>   And nearer than hands or feet."

In Buddhism you have a commentary on the most pessimistic book in the Bible, the Book of Ecclesiastes. Without Christ, and without hope of a resurrection, all is indeed vanity and vexation of spirit. In Mohammedanism you have the old truth of the prophets of Israel, the transcendence of God, and His sovereign irresistible will in the history of the world and of all humanity. In fact many great truths are held in common with Christianity, and are held with zeal and devotion.

But it is not difficult to show that Christ and, therefore, Christianity, stand supreme, unique, and final in ten great particulars; and we are able to give an answer to every man who asks for the reason of the hope that is in us.

(1) First of all, Christ's Bible—I mean the Bible His mother opened to Him and read to Him at Nazareth—and our New Testament, both of them teach *the unity and the solidarity of the human race*. You do not find that in any other sacred book. From the first chapter of Genesis until the last chapter of the New Testament it is always one great human family. And if we had only the 67th Psalm we would have there the foundation for a great league of all nations. Paul, standing on Mars' Hill, said very clearly : " God hath made of one blood (of one substance) the whole human family."

Then you turn to the Epistles, and you find that solidarity imbedded deep in the theology. " As in Adam, so in Christ—" united for ever in the image of God which was lost, and brought together again in the image of God that is to be restored. John in his Apocalyptic vision said : " Lo, a great multitude which no man can number, of all nations, and kindreds, and peoples, and tongues, stood before the Throne, and before the Lamb."

Where else than in the Bible do you find such marvellous phraseology on the solidarity of the human race ? I tried for the fourth time to read the Bhagavad Gita, the New Testament of Hinduism, and I found in it the narrow caste system of Hinduism, and the doctrine of incarnations, but nothing of the universal, or of the race as a whole.

(2) *Jesus Christ is the only religious leader Who came to destroy all race barriers and class hatreds*. He is adequate for this if we will only give Him His right of way. He came to destroy the racial chasm, and build the bridge of human brotherhood. He gave woman her true place ; childhood its rights ; the slave his freedom ; the barbarian welcome. Lecky, in his history of European morals, gives the evidence of this gradual development.

Take the words of the Apostle Paul ; and the more you meditate on them the more you see that here you have the Magna

Charta of Christianity, equality in Jesus Christ. "Neither Jew nor Greek, male nor female, bond nor free, Roman nor barbarian." After nineteen centuries we are still far behind these lofty standards of the international mind of the Apostle Paul. The life of Jesus Christ is a rebuke to all Nordic, or American, or Anglo-Saxon pride, and all our miserable race prejudices and class hatreds.

(3) *Jesus Christ, the Founder of Christianity, is the Son of Man, of mankind.* He is not the Son of any nation. The Son of Man was His own favourite title. What does it mean? He is the ideal Man, the ideal of humanity, the ideal of all the ages, and of the whole human race.

When you read the life of Mohammed you say : There stands an ideal Arab in thought, in life, in outlook. When you read the life of Confucius you say : There is a true Chinese, the scholar and gentleman of Chinese civilisation. When you read the life of Buddha you say : There you have an Indian ascetic and mystic ; but his pathway is wholly Asiatic. When you read the life of Socrates you say : Here is the greatest Greek philosopher ; but he always remained a Greek. But when you turn over the pages of the Gospel, and look at the face of Jesus, you find that He was neither Occidental nor Oriental, neither Jew nor Greek; He was the Alpha and the Omega of ideal manhood and ideal womanhood.

He has all the virtues which we admire in the Oriental, and none of the faults and the vices which we despise in the Occidental. Patience, courtesy, and hospitality—these are the supreme virtues of the East. And as you read the Gospels you find such virtues supreme in Jesus Christ. Truth, honesty, and moral courage—those are the virtues of the Nordic races; and Jesus Christ was the acme of them all. The only Man Who was not a moral coward in Holy Week was Jesus Christ. His disciples forsook Him and fled. Pilate was a coward. But Christ had the great moral courage to say to His disciples, even in the Garden of Gethsemane: " Arise, let us go hence "—toward the Cross!

(4) *Christ's life and purpose and commands and promises are world-wide.* They are adapted to and adequate for the whole human family. This is a unique characteristic of Old Testament prophecy and New Testament teaching not found in any

other religion—the note of universalism. Christ's marching orders were universal; His triumph was to be absolute. "Every knee shall bow to Him."

No other religion ever held out such a world-wide programme. You find nothing of it in Buddhism, or Hinduism, or Zoroastrianism. Their golden age is always in the past; our golden age is in the future. The watchword of missions, the evangelisation of the whole world, is absolutely inconceivable except for Christianity.

(5) *Christ's laws and rituals are possible everywhere for everybody*. They are adequate for all, because He is our contemporary. Jesus offers to men, women, and children, a ritual and worship that excludes none but the impenitent. Christ's words to the poor Samaritan woman are still ringing down the centuries: "God is a Spirit, and they that worship Him must worship Him in spirit and in truth." Men need no local shrine as in Mecca; no sacred river, as at Benares; no sacred mountain, no sacred city. Prayer to Him can be offered everywhere in every place by every one.

And the observance of the Sacraments which Christ instituted is as possible in the

THE SOLITARY THRONE 21

catacombs as in the cathedrals, in a hut as in a palace, in a prison, or in the trenches. There you may break the bread, and receive from His hands the tokens of His dying love. It is the only religion whose Founder could have said, and ever did say: "Suffer the little children to come unto Me." Mohammed never said it, and had he said it they would not have gone to him. And as for the Indian religions, the Brahmin priesthood marries little girls to the gods of lust instead of inviting them to the bosom of the Saviour.

(6) *We have a Book that has been translated and is translatable into all languages, and for all humanity.* Other sacred books are not altogether translatable. Their style and contents make it impossible to translate the sacred books, so-called, of the East. The Ko-ji-ki is the sacred book of the Shinto religion; but the American scholar who translated it apologised in the preface that large sections of it were so indecent that it had to be put into Latin. The Hindu volumes on the Tantric Yogi festival could not be translated for public reading; nor could three certain chapters of the Koran, perhaps more, be read in a mixed audience.

But the Bible, although it speaks frankly of sin, retains the purity and simplicity of its message in all the nine hundred languages into which it has been translated; and each year there are fourteen new languages added. It is the best selling book in the world; and thirty-three million copies are sold in one year.

(7) *Jesus Christ has continued to occupy the dominant place in the world of law, culture, and morals,* a solitary throne. Pilate's inscription is fulfilled before our eyes—" Jesus, the King of the Jews "—because He is the King of international law (Latin), the King of culture (Greek), the King of ethics (Hebrew). His Kingdom is an everlasting Kingdom. His law is acknowledged as an international ideal.

In the expression of human culture through music, sculpture, painting, architecture, poetry—their highest inspiration, as asserted earlier, has been found in Jesus Christ. All the world has gone after Him. His ethics are the yardstick by which we measure others, and by which others measure us. By the suffrage rights of humanity Jesus Christ is elected King of hearts. His love is winning the whole world.

The world population, according to Dr.

THE SOLITARY THRONE 23

Hume, of Union Theological Seminary, is made up as follows : Zoroastrians, 100,000 ; Shintos, 24,000,000 ; Tacists, 43,000,000 ; Buddhists, 137,000,000 ; Mohammedans, 240,000,000 ; Confucianists, 250,000,000 ; Hindus, 217,000,000, and those who profess and call themselves Christians, however far apart we may be, and however distantly we may follow Him, number 588,000,000, twice as many as the followers of any other religion.

(8) *Christianity is unique and alone in its conception of God and of Christ's revelation of God* ; and it is the highest and most comprehensive. Islam says that God is transcendent, above all. Hinduism says that God is immanent. Polytheism says that gods are incarnate ; that you can hold them to your bosom. Jesus Christ reveals God as all three of these. The Father of infinite majesty ; the Holy Spirit Who broods over creation—Who dwells in human hearts ; and the Son of His love Who was made flesh, and dwelt among us, on Whose bosom John could lean, and Who could say : " No man hath seen God at any time ; the only begotten Son, which is in the bosom of the Father, He hath declared Him." " Have I been so long time with you, and yet hast

thou not known Me, Philip? He that hath seen Me hath seen the Father."

Christ is the Alpha and Omega of all we know about God, the Father. All other conceptions of Deity are in comparison nebulous, vague, distant, or distorted. Once, while riding along a country road in China in company with a Chinese missionary, Charles Ogilvie, I put a question to him as to what Confucius taught about God, and he said this in answer: "A child in our Sunday School knows more about God than all you can find in all the Analects of Confucius." Without God, without hope; because without Christ.

(9) *Jesus Christ combined in Himself the highest ideal of character and of redemption.* " Behold the Lamb of God!" How spotless, and yet sufficient as an atonement for all human guilt! No religion ever caught that idea. Prayer and sacrifice are found in all the world among all nations. There is sacrifice and propitiation in all the religions, but they never rise to the sacrifice and propitiation that you find in John 3. 16.

> "Not all the blood of beasts
>   On Jewish altars slain,
> Can give the guilty conscience peace,
>   Or wash away its stain."

The Solitary Throne

Peter puts it for us—" Who His own self bare our sins in His own body on the tree." " Hallelujah, what a Saviour ! "—a Saviour Who is " very God of very God, begotten not made." He came down to the manger to lift us up, and to set us poor sinners as princes in His Kingdom.

(10) *Christ offers the strongest proof for the truth of His message; namely, experience.* And it is thus that we sing " All hail the power of Jesus' Name ! " In accord with our scientific age, and the demands of the laboratory, Jesus Christ appeals to those very tests. For Christianity is not a religion of human authority, like Confucianism. It is not a religion of tradition, like Judaism. It is not a religion of force and might, like Islam. It is not a religion based upon argument and philosophy; although Christianity is a philosophy, and although the Bible calls upon us to reason with God. But it is a religion, first and always, from beginning to end, of experiment and experience; it is a pragmatic faith. " Oh, taste and see that the Lord is gracious ! " " Prove Me now herewith, saith the Lord, and see if I will not pour you out such a blessing that there shall not be room enough to receive it." " Come

unto Me all ye that labour, and are heavy laden, and I will give you rest." "Ask, and it shall be given you." "Seek, and ye shall find." "Knock, and it shall be opened unto you."

Now, no scientist could speak in more definite terms than those. George Romanes, the great English scientist, was once a sceptic, and then he came face to face with John 7. 17 : " If any man will do His will, he shall know of the doctrine." His biographer tells us that from that text he found his way to a simple faith in Jesus Christ. When you and I face Jesus Christ we are conscious, with Isaiah and Paul and Peter, of our own absolute spiritual bankruptcy.

When, at the Jerusalem Conference, we were spending days in discussing the spiritual values of the non-Christian religions, a speaker representing the Dutch Bible Society asserted that they possessed *no* spiritual values judged by the gold standard of the religion of Christ. The experiment tried for twenty centuries by hundreds of millions has never yet failed. We are all spiritually bankrupt before Christ ; but immediately after that experiment the position is reversed. We become

THE SOLITARY THRONE 27

affluent with all the riches of Jesus Christ, His perfect righteousness, imputed and imparted to us by His Holy Spirit.

This is the religion which we preach and commend to the non-Christian world. Christ occupies the solitary throne of every heart once yielded to Him; even as He occupies the throne of Heaven, before which myriads of those who have been redeemed are falling prostrate before Him, crying: " Holy, Holy, Holy! Unto Him that loved us and loosed us from our sins, to Him be the glory for ever!" The Lamb is on the Throne now and to all eternity.

I want to close with two quotations; one from Professor MacIntosh, of Edinburgh, on " *The Originality of the Christian Message ;*" and the other from Pascal.

Professor MacIntosh says : " Any faith which challenges the finality of Christianity must produce the equivalent of Jesus Christ. He . . . embodies the Gospel in Himself, and in Him its own finality, if real, must be found. To call Christianity the absolute or final religion, therefore, is to contend not merely that, in Jesus Christ, God is presented in a form higher and more spiritually satisfying than elsewhere, but that the relationship to the Father on which believers thus enter is such that it cannot be transcended."

Pascal, the great French Christian, says in his "*Thoughts on Religion*" : "Jesus Christ is the centre of everything and the object of everything; and he who does not know Him knows nothing of the order of the world and nothing of himself. In Him is all our felicity and virtue, our life, our light, our hope ; apart from Him there is nothing but vice, misery, darkness, despair, and we see only obscurity, and confusion in the nature of God and in our own." How can we withhold such a Saviour from a dying world ? How shall we escape if we neglect to proclaim so great a salvation ? Then let us proclaim for " how shall they hear without a preacher ? "

II

His Ministers a Flame

II

His Ministers a Flame

IN all nations and in all ages men have associated fire with God's presence and with God's power. From the earliest times in nearly every country men have said, or whispered: "Our God is a consuming fire."

You find fire-worship as one of the earliest forms of communion with the Deity. It is in Mexico, and Japan, and India, and Persia, and the Islands of the Sea. In the Bible, over four hundred times in the Old Testament, and seventy-five times in the New Testament; fire is associated with the appearance, the manifestation, the power, the symbolism of Deity.

Now Paul uses a word here, which brings us right into the midst of our subject: "*anazopūrein.*" And the word he uses in the Greek Testament is only used once in the New Testament, twice in the entire Bible. It is used once in Timothy, and once in Genesis, and means to kindle or fan into flame. To Timothy,

Paul says: "Kindle again the flame that came to you from the ignition power of God's Holy Spirit that has died down on the altar of your life."

That Greek word contains three different words. Putting life into the flame or fire. It occurs in that beautiful chapter where the gifts come from Joseph to old Jacob, and the Septuagint versions says that when Jacob saw the chariots, his heart kindled up again.

My theme is that process of the kindling of the fire in the hearts of God's servants, that we may serve Him as ministers who are aflame, on fire. Obviously when you strike a match, when you kindle a fire on the hearth, even when you start the engine of your motor three things take place. There is the spark of ignition; there is the process of combustion, which is always sacrificial; and there is the resultant illumination and the spiritual dynamic. To put it spiritually: the spark of faith that ignites; the process of combustion which is sacrificial; and the resultant illumination and the spiritual dynamic which never take place without the sacrificial process of combustion.

Now that kind of terminology is not the

language of Canaan. It was not the language of Keswick fifty years ago. But it is right up-to-date. It smacks of the laboratory, the factory, and the garage. Ignition, power, light, motion, heat.

First of all Paul speaks to Timothy about the spark that kindled the flame in the heart of that dear son of his whom he loved, and for whom he prayed day and night.

Every life is waiting for that kindling spark. Men are dead in trespasses and sins : and though the altar of our youthful prayers may have been broken down, and the sacrifice of our lives once made at Confirmation, or in the Sunday School, may have been drenched in the cold water of heartless criticism thrice over, yet the God of Elijah can send His fire on the altar ; and we all know whence that fire comes ; it comes only from God.

That gift, as Paul says, was " bestowed on thee with the laying on of my hands ; " but it was not the hands of Paul ; it was the fire of Christ in the heart of Timothy. Of course there is a sense, as all fathers and mothers know, in which grace is hereditary. It is not heresy to believe this, because in our hymnary we have that beautiful hymn by Horatius Bonar, where he says : " I thank Thee for a godly ancestry."

"From thy infancy," says Paul to Timothy, "thou hast known the Holy Scriptures which are able to make thee wise unto salvation." That is, from his earliest youth Timothy carried a very tinder-box in his soul, put there by his mother and his grandmother. And Paul is absolutely certain that his mother's faith and prayer, and his grandmother's covenant intercession are going to be fulfilled ; their intercession cannot be in vain. That is a great passage for us who are fathers or grandfathers to lay hold of.

It surely cannot be true of the rising generation that the prayers of fathers and mothers of past generations are not going to be answered by the God who keepeth covenant unto a thousand generations. Paul's ideal for flaming manhood is that of a youth whose mind is aflame with the truth of God ; whose heart is aflame with love for humanity ; and whose will is set on fire with a passion for God's righteousness in an age of iniquity.

First of all he tells us, as we all know here, that ignition is the gift of God in thee,

His Ministers a Flame

His alone. One spark from the eternal fire, and our life changes. "Only believe, and thou shalt see, that God is all in all to thee."

Paul says that because he himself experienced it on the road to Damascus; and because he believes that Timothy somewhere and somehow at some time in his life experienced the same miracle of ignition —that Christ lives in him, as Christ lives in Paul—then for Timothy to live and for Paul to live is not money, or pleasure, or honour, or power, or ease, but for him to live is Christ.

Now we have heard so much about ignition, about power, about the new life in our hymns and preaching, that we have forgotten what it means when we glibly ask for the baptism of fire. Because after ignition there always comes combustion, and the process that takes place after that ignition is always sacrificial. You cannot keep your wood pile, you cannot keep your coal in the cellar, if you would have a fire on the hearth. Remember the words of our Lord Jesus Christ: "John was a burning and a shining light." The burning must come before the shining.

Many of our younger ministers and

theological students expect to have the shining without the burning; and that is utterly impossible. There can be no power and no light and no heat without the sacrifice of the altar. "I come to cast fire on the earth, and how am I straitened until it be kindled," said the Lord Jesus. Fire is a marvellous thing both in nature and in grace.

A man set on fire is an apostle of his age. And the only one who can kindle the spark of light and fire on the hearth where it has died down is He Who has revealed Himself as the God of fire, our Lord Jesus Christ. "Our God is a consuming fire."

The last picture we have of Jesus Christ in the Bible is not the one we show to the children in the Sunday School. The last picture of Jesus Christ in the Bible is that portrait of Him that cannot be put on canvas; it is there on the first page of the Book of the Revelation—a portrait of "Prometheus Unbound." John says: "I saw one like the Son of Man; His eyes were as a flame of fire, the shining of His face as the sun in his strength, His feet as brass burning in a furnace." You cannot picture this on canvas.

His Ministers a Flame

"He held seven stars in His right hand, walking amid the seven burning golden candlesticks, a new Prometheus with fire from Heaven (unbound)."

Christ in all His symbolic Divine glory came to cast fire on the earth. And how is He straitened until His ministers, you and I, become a flame of fire? What else should they be?

What is the process of combustion? When you strike a match, when you light a fire on the hearth, when you start a great fire in a factory, when you turn on the power of your motor engine, there are five things that always take place. First of all, *fire always tears asunder and binds together*. Fire separates and it unites. "I am come to set at variance." "A man's foes shall be those of his own household."

Who can fully explain the chemical, the divisive action of combustion? The law of cleavage that takes place when the wood and the coal are torn asunder in the flame, when the oxygen and carbon and hydrogen are set free. You cannot explain that. No more can you explain what takes place when Christ says to someone: "Forsake all and follow Me." The flame and heat either ends in electricity and light and power, or they end in smoke and ashes and death.

Tell me, is your ministry a burning and shining light, or a smoking flax-wick, slowly dying out to ashes? Think how the fire of Christ tears asunder and separates. Think of the intolerance of Jesus; His divisive demands; His stern rebukes; His sevenfold woe to the Pharisees of His day. That was His conference address in Matt. 23. It would stir all great Conferences to-day if we dared to use those words in regard to ourselves, and to each other, which Christ used in regard to the ministry of the Jewish Church.

The very presence of Jesus always demands decision. He always divides and cleaves mankind, eternally, horizontally, and perpendicularly; to the right; to the left. The highest Heaven; the lowest Hell. Separation from God. In Christ—joy and peace; without Christ—without hope and without God.

At a Convention, when Jesus comes something happens, as when He was at Capernaum. Luke tells us that a *great* multitude followed Him. "And Jesus turned and said unto them, Except a man forsake all that he hath ... Except a man hate his father and mother, yes, and his own life also, he cannot be My disciple." And when He comes again in glory He will manifest that sundering, that tearing power of the flaming fire of His eye. " Come ye blessed of My Father . . . Depart from Me ye cursed."

You say, " That was Jesus ! " Well, consider Paul. If anyone ever was a flame of fire, it was Paul. He wrote to the Corinthian Church : " Come ye out from among them, and be ye separate." " What fellowship hath light with darkness ? " We are always giving the Benediction of the Second Epistle to the Corinthians ; but no minister dares to pronounce that sentence in the 1st Epistle : " If any man love not the Lord Jesus Christ let him be Anathema."

> "I thought His love would weaken
>   As more and more He knew me,
> But it burneth like a beacon,
>   And its light and heat go through me."

" I came to cast fire on the earth." Christ speaks to us, with His eyes like a flame of fire. May God forgive us, for when we speak in His Name we are often so cold, so lukewarm ; so unconscious of that baptism of separation which was given to us ministers by the laying on of hands—the true apostolic succession. " Ours the mighty ordination of the Pierced Hand." " How hard it is to be a Christian," says Robert Browning; and how hard to be a preacher.

And then *fire unites things that are broken asunder*. It welds together into one, things that belong together. There is nothing that binds like fire. As you drive through the Black Country, and go through the Birmingham and Wolverhampton districts, the smoke of those countless chimneys tell us how marvellous is the binding power of fire in steel manufacture.

So all our race problems in the United States and South Africa, all our class hatred in Britain, or Germany, or anywhere else, all our ecclesiastical disputes and differences, and our most unhappy divisions, would be healed and dissolved if we were only brought close to Christ, and entered into the crucible of His love. Our sectarian divisions and parochial prejudices disappear as soon as we enter the fire. Carping criticisms of fellow Christians become impossible in the presence of Christ; and where He is we are " all one in Christ Jesus."

Any doctrine of the Holy Spirit, or

of sanctification, that fails to teach tolerance of fellow Christians, and love of all the brethren, I tell you solemnly that I believe it is a false fire; it does not come from God's Spirit. When He unites us it is like the bell-metal which comes from the crucible in a real unity.

In a great factory I once saw them putting into the furnace the copper, the iron, the tin, and the brass; and they all came out melted into a new substance, vocal with celestial harmony and heavenly music, and it became the call to worship. It had been through the fire.

In the crucible of Christ's love there is neither "Jew nor Greek, bond nor free, male nor female, neither east nor west. We are all one in Christ Jesus." It is a good thing to confess that one article of the Apostle's Creed, which is believed by all the Churches, and is more transgressed against than any article of the Creed: "I believe in the communion of saints." "I believe in the forgiveness of sins"—all sorts of ecclesiastical sins. "And in the life everlasting."

Some one has said we will see a great many people in Heaven that we never expected to see, and they will hold a place of honour higher than ourselves. " I believe in the Communion of saints." In that fire-baptism we all become one in Christ, a Christian unity that is not artificial but supernatural.

Again Paul says to Timothy : " Stir into flame the gift that is in thee," because *fire purifies*. Jesus is the crucible of character. Malachi tells us that " He, the Messiah, shall sit as a Refiner and Purifier of silver; He shall purify the sons of Levi, and purge them." That is, it begins on the platform; it begins with the ministers, the Christian leaders. The Roman Catholic Church believes in Purgatory hereafter. We believe in Purgatory now.

All meanness, all hatred, all envy, all impurity, all criticism, all suspicion, all jealousy that is in your heart or mine will disappear if we just throw them into the crucible of Christ's loving soul. And when He stirs into the flame our intellect and emotions and will, to be His true disciples, we become ministers that are a flame of fire. The process of combustion tears asunder, and it binds together, it solders as nothing else can.

His Ministers a Flame

But the flame does a destructive work also ; because *fire destroys and consumes.* You remember those days in the War, when you saw outside the great camps those mighty incinerators built for the army, and which existed for no other purpose than to destroy and to put away for ever everything that was unclean in the soldiers' camp. All that was hygienically impure, all the dross, went up in smoke. So with our lives. We have the promise that the fire will destroy all the mistakes and the follies of our lives, all the failures of our Christian ministry, all the wood and the hay and the stubble, all the dregs of our regret ; they will all go up in smoke, and the silver and the gold and the precious stones will abide for ever. David said it for us on his knees : " Thou knowest my foolishness, and my sins are not hid from Thee."

One of the most interesting, traditional, apocryphal sayings of Jesus is this—and why should it not be true ?—" He that is near Me is near the fire." Lord Tennyson was very fond of that saying, and loved to meditate on it. And perhaps Paul knew that apocryphal saying of Jesus when he told Timothy to fan into flame all his spiritual gifts. Our hymn speaks of it:

> "Spirit of God, descend upon my heart,
>   Ween it from earth, through all its pulses move,
> Stoop to my weakness, mighty as Thou art,
>   And make me love Thee as I ought to love.
>
> "Teach me to love Thee as Thine angels love,
>   One holy passion filling all my frame.
> The baptism of the Heaven-descended Dove,
>   My heart an altar, and Thy love the flame."

Again, *fire always gives energy*. Huxley, that great scientist, tells you what takes place in the world of energy when you simply light a tallow candle. Every one of us is to be like that of which the children sing, "A little candle burning in the night, you in your small corner, and I in mine." Such fires give energy, the very dynamic of God. "I can do all things through Christ which strengtheneth me."

The Holy Spirit is the wisdom of God and the power of God, because the Holy Spirit is the fire of God. And wherever there is this energy of fire it spreads; that is the characteristic of all fire. That is why children love to play with fire. That is why every sensible man is afraid of the danger of fire—the prairie fire, the great conflagration. The flame that separates, unites, consumes, also energises

HIS MINISTERS A FLAME 45

and spreads until it becomes a great conflagration. What a glorious symbolism of the Acts of the Apostles, beginning at Jerusalem, and spreading through Judea and Samaria, and on unto the uttermost parts of the earth!

It took the Church eighteen hundred years to reach the uttermost part of the earth—one hundred and eighty degrees from Jerusalem—and now we hear of revivals in China, in India, in Uganda, and all around the globe; the fire is still spreading. That flame came down at Pentecost.

I love to go to the University Library in Princeton. Over the fireplace in the library of that Graduate School there are carved these Latin words from the Vulgate Psalter: "*In Meditatione mea exardescet ignis.*" " While I sit meditating, the fire burns." What a motto to have in a university library! " While I sat musing the fire burned." Yes, it burns. But what fire is it that burns as we sit meditating? For there are fires celestial, and fires terrestrial, and fires infernal. As James puts it: " Behold, how great a forest is kindled by how small a fire! And the tongue is a fire "—the tongue of speech, or the tongue in the printed page; the tongue of the righteous and the tongue of the wicked. One is fanned with the flame of Heaven; the other burns with the blaze of Hell. The one is as the shining light that shineth more and more unto the perfect day. And the other is like a wandering star to which is reserved the blackness of darkness for ever and ever.

"While I was musing," said David, "the fire burned." Yes, it burned into David's deepest soul, so that he gave us the seven Penitential Psalms as well as the Hallelujah Chorus and the 103rd Psalm of thanksgiving. As Kipling puts it in his couplet:

> "Down to Jehennom, or up to the Throne
> He travels the fastest who travels alone."

When you are sitting meditating you may be quite sure the fires are burning. And when we speak, God grant that our tongues may be always celestial fires, and not terrestrial, or infernal fires that burn on the hearth of our souls.

And, lastly there is *the dynamic of such a flaming ministry*. I preached this sermon in America on a certain occasion when I had to travel by train on the Saturday night. I put one question to the conductor

HIS MINISTERS A FLAME

of the train. I said to him : " Do you think that the professors and students at Princeton are flames of fire ? " He smiled, and said : " No, I do not think so." That was enough for me to think over. The impression that a minister makes on a railway guard is not that of a flame of fire.

Once I was to preach a sermon at an anniversary in a Methodist Church ; there were a great number of ministers present, and I was greatly honoured to be allowed to preach there. We met in the vestry. And the sexton, whose work it was to take care of the comfort of the preacher, said to me : " Would you like a glass of water in the pulpit ? " I said : " No, I would like *a bonfire*." He smiled. That is what I felt that day.

It is a strange custom that we should supply a minister with a glass of water ; if only we could supply him with a bonfire in the pulpit, a spiritual bonfire. I felt I needed one that morning ; it would have been a great help to me.

We need the dynamic of a flaming ministry that will set the Church on fire. In the Acts of the Apostles we find the divine capacities, the supernatural dynamic issuing from the lives of ordinary men, fanning the faith into flame.

The New Testament teaches us that all spiritual energy, every kind of spiritual power comes from one primary source, the Holy Spirit of God. Apart from Him we can do nothing. He is the overflowing fountain of life and light. " Apart from Me ye can do nothing," says Christ. " He that believeth in Me, the works that I do, shall he do also : and greater works than these shall he do because I go to My Father."

That is the hardest text in the Bible to try to understand. Yet when we meditate upon it, and think of the work of Hudson Taylor, of David Livingstone, of Horace Underwood—to mention only three missionaries among thousands, their work was far greater in area than the work of Jesus Christ ; it was far greater in results than the visible results of our Lord's work during His three years' ministry ; far greater in length of time, far greater in proportion to their strength than the miracles of Jesus Christ. " He that believeth in Me, the works that I do shall he do also, and greater works than these shall he do because I go to My Father."

Let us often read the Acts of the

Apostles. It is a neglected Book amongst those who ought to be leaders of the Church of Christ. You can label its chapters, " The Acts of the Apostles—God's Book of Fire." Then you can put on the different chapters : Ignition ; Combustion ; Dynamic ; Illumination ; Conflagration—it is all there.

What matchless courage against all opposition. What patience in defeat ! What love for all humanity ! What bursting through barriers of race-prejudice and class-hatred ! What discipline of self in an age of self-indulgence in Rome and Greece ! They preached the pure life, a pure womanhood, and a pure manhood. What boldness in proclaiming a message that was to the world-wise of their day the acme of foolishness, and to the Jewish Church a perpetual stumbling-block ! Yet with it they turned the world upside down—intellectually, socially, and morally, and all in one generation.

I recall the words of Von Harnack : " About the year 50 A.D., Christianity was an ellipse whose foci were Jerusalem and Antioch. Fifty years later these foci were Ephesus and Rome. The colossal change implied in this proves the greatness of Paul's work, and of the work done by the first Christian missionaries." By then the empire of Cæsar had become the empire of Another, even Jesus Christ our Lord. And the astonishing fact is that these laws of spiritual ignition, of combustion, of dynamic, are *semper, ubique, et ab omnibus*, the same always, everywhere, for all. May God grant unto us their fulfilment! May we never glibly pray the prayer that we may be filled with the Holy Spirit.

I shall never forget my own professor under whom I was taught theology a man some fifty years ago telling to stop as he prayed that prayer; and the man stopped in the middle of his petition. "John," he said, "do you know what it might mean to your father and mother, to your home-ties, and to your whole life, if you were really baptised with the Holy Spirit?" When we pray that prayer, it means combustion—sacrifice; "my heart an altar, and Thy love the flame."

"A great multitude followed Jesus, and He turned and said: Except a man hate his father and mother, yea, and his own life also, he cannot be My disciple." You have it illustrated at every baptismal service in India, in Persia, in Arabia, in China, where people who follow Christ are called upon to forsake all for the love of our Lord. Shall we not pray : " Fan into flame that little spark which God has kindled in our souls by His grace ? "

III

Photophobia

III
Photophobia

WHEN a patient is in an opthalmic hospital and prefers darkness rather than light, prefers the dark shadows rather than the brightness of the sun, the physicians call it photophobia.

It is hard to be a Christian, because all of us at some time, and some of us all the time, are suffering from photophobia. You will remember the word, for you have other words in the English language written in the same way. A photograph is a writing made by the light in the camera. Hydrophobia is when a dog is afraid to drink—the symptom of a serious disease. Anglophobia is where the nations are afraid of Great Britain. So you will remember these two simple Greek words, and you will not forget the subject, which is Photophobia. By photophobia we mean fear of the light ; an intolerance of that which is natural and beautiful. This is a strange paradox that seems contradictory to the very laws of nature, the laws of life, the laws of beauty, and which occurs, nevertheless, in exceptional cases among plants and animals, as if it were a parable of spiritual photophobia.

There are mosses in the depths of the dark forests of Africa, there are certain algæ and seaweed in the depths of the ocean, which seem to grow best where the sun never shines. So the owl is the bird of the night, while the eagle greets the daybreak. The mole lives underground and hides from the sunlight. And in the Mammoth Cave, Kentucky, there are thousands of fishes that have lost their sight because they have lived in the darkness for so long. The eyeball and the organ remains, but for centuries they have propagated in the darkness.

Now in man photophobia is always a symptom of serious disease. It is assocated sometimes with colour-blindness; but it is always present in disease of the iris, or the cornea. I have often seen in our hospitals in Arabia, poor Arab children suffering from this malady. How they would huddle in a dark corner, or bury their faces in a dirty pillow, afraid of the light. There is not usually much pain, but the doctor knows that it is an indication, a symptom of a

PHOTOPHOBIA 57

very serious eye-disease. Which things are a parable of the spiritual world.

The story is told by John in the words of Jesus. " Now there was a man of the Pharisees named Nicodemus, a ruler of the Jews. The same came to Jesus by night." He had no photophobia ; he was groping towards the light, an earnest seeker after God, not far from the truth. He said: " We know Thou art a teacher come from God." And to this earnest enquirer, who, for fear of the Jews, came to Jesus by night, our Blessed Saviour unfolded the very heart of the Gospel, the very heart of God.

To Nicodemus He declared the necessity and the mystery of the second birth. He told him the heavenly things of the Incarnation, and the Atonement with all that it involved, of Christ's twofold nature and twofold state as Man and God, of humiliation and exaltation. This chapter contains the whole theology and Christology of the Gospel. " Verily, verily, I say unto you . . . No one hath ascended into Heaven, but He that descended out of Heaven, even the Son of Man, Who is in Heaven." Out of Heaven He came, into Heaven He went, and in Heaven He is for you and for me and for Nicodemus ; the love that would not let humanity go to eternal perdition, but saved men through the Cross on which Christ was lifted up, even as Moses lifted up the brazen serpent in the wilderness.

That love He explains to Nicodemus in the words that follow. He said to Nicodemus: You are a ruler of the Jews, you cannot understand the principles of salvation, the laws of the kingdom of darkness and the kingdom of light. He that believes is saved. He that refuses to believe, refuses to look toward the uplifted One, is judged by his own act. How can he escape if he neglect so great a salvation? If Christ had not come, they would have had no sin, but now they have no cloak for their sin; and the reason for this crisis and judgment, for this condemnation lies in one stupendous fact, the Incarnation; the manifestation of God's love in sending His Son into the world.

Since the Coming of Christ and the exhibition of God's love in a perfect human life, in the light of that holiness and that love of the Father, and because men have seen His face, human sin is no longer the result of ignorance, but of deliberate choice and preference. The world's secret sins are now set "in the light of His countenance."

That is what Paul explains in the 1st chapter of his Epistle to the Romans. The heathen are not only to be pitied, and, God knows, they *are* to be pitied; the Mohammedans are not only to be had compassion on, but we are to see that they are under condemnation, because they do not love the light. This is the crisis of history, and of the biography of every human soul, that light is come into the world, that true Light that lighteth every man, the Light that is the light of man.

I would like to ask three questions in view of the fact that you and I once upon a time blindfolded Jesus; and once upon a time, or here and now, are suffering from photophobia.

1. What is the *nature* ?—2. What is the *cause* ?—3. What is the *cure*—of this terrible disease of the soul ?

Now what is *the nature of photophobia?* " Men love darkness rather than light, because their deeds are evil," and thus the fact of photophobia, of men hating the light and loving the darkness, is patent to all of us. No one who is engaged in what is called " the cure of souls "—a beautiful word—but knows that this is one of the distinguishing symptoms of a man who is without Christ, and without hope, and without God.

It was so in the days of Jesus. The historical and experimental background of the story in the 3rd of chapter John is evidence of it. They hated Jesus without cause. "He came unto His own, and His own received Him not." Once they led Him to the brow of the hill at Nazareth. Once we read that "many walked no more with Him." And at last we read : "They all forsook Him and fled." And He turned, and with tears in His eyes, said : " Ye will not come unto Me that ye might have life." The record is in the prophecy of Isaiah that " He was despised and rejected of men." The record in the Gospel is that they mocked Him, and spat upon Him, and disowned Him, and blindfolded Him.

There is no tragedy more real and more moving in all history, and in our own lives, than the deliberate rejection of Christ ; because it is due, not to any extraordinary wickedness in the Jews, or the Romans, or the people of New York, or the people of London, but to the ordinary motives of men. In the case of *the Sadducees*, there was the family of Annas and Caiaphas ; their rejection was due to selfish determination to uphold by all means their own precarious position of authority, dignity, and wealth under the Roman sovereignty, and to suppress every movement that might possibly make the Romans jealous. And so they hated " the Light of the World."

With *the Pharisees* it was due to their refusal (at the bidding of one who was in their eyes only a layman from Nazareth) to acknowledge their own profound mistakes and ignorance, and to think over again the prophecies to which Christ pointed and the real meaning of the religion of Abraham, of which they were the orthodox representatives. In the case of the mass of *the people*, who cried, " Crucify Him ! " it was due to their worldly pre-occupation of mind and their stubborn nationalism, which made them entertain wild hopes, and blinded them to the spiritual way of redemption which Jesus kept on preaching to them in spite of their hardness of heart.

Now these three classes of people are still with us to-day. They crucified our Lord on Calvary nineteen hundred years ago, and they crucify Him afresh to-day. The spiritual pride of Annas ; the self-righteousness of Caiaphas ; the love of Mammon in Judas ; the secular cynicism of Pilate—

all these were there, and all these together crucified Jesus Christ.

The enemies of Jesus to-day are not those outside the Churches altogether. We who attempt to be spiritual physicians know full well that photophobia is found in the pews of our Churches; and sometimes it is found in the case of those who stand in the pulpit. It is found in our own hearts. We read : " They blindfolded Him." That was the climax in the career of those who loved darkness rather than light.

Did it ever occur to you to ask yourself why they blindfolded Jesus? Was it because His eyes were filled with such a holy wonder at their unbelief? Was it because His eyes looked down on them with such compassion, and yet such condemnation of their wilful ignorance, flashing with a light that smote their consciences like a flame of fire? They could not bear to look into His face, and so, Mark tells us, some began to spit upon Him, others covered His face and began to buffet Him. Luke puts it very briefly. He says : " They blindfolded Him."

Their cowardice was only matched by their hatred. They smote Him; they mocked Him; they then asked for a proof of His divinity. The Jewish mob, when they could not hide their faces, covered His face, shutting out the light not from Jesus, but from their own hearts. And so it is to-day.

There are three manifestations of Christ in the world which every one who is not of the light fears, avoids, and tries to cover up. (1) You have the Christ of History, the " Light of the World "—Jesus. (2) You have the revealed Word of God—Christ in the Old Testament, and in the clear record of the Gospels. That Light has been translated into over nine hundred languages, in order that in every speech and language, across every land and continent, men, if they will, can see the face of Jesus. (3) And there is the light of His Holy Catholic Church. " Ye are the light of the world "—in spite of all our faults, and divisions, and failures.

No one can say that where there is one single Christian who walks in the light, his neighbours and friends cannot see, at least, a dim reflection of that light that never was on sea or land, covering the whole universe with its glory.

This threefold light lighteth every man that cometh into the world to-day. Christ, the Bible, the Church, are in all lands, and before all eyes to-day. On the radio, on the front page of the newspapers, in the hands of every colporteur, beside each cot in every hospital, on the foreign field—the Light of the World is Jesus. This Jesus has become an unescapable fact—the fact of Christ. Jesus rises above all the peaks of human history, like Everest of the Himalayas, far above all the foot-hills and mountains. There He stands, sovereign, supreme. Every man in any land knows that who has ever read the life of Jesus. Yet men have always been afraid, and, therefore, unwilling to look Christ in the face. They try to escape the Jesus of history by declaring that the story is only a myth; or they refuse to look at the full portrait of Christ in the Gospels; they whittle away the Gospels until there is only a small proportion of them left, and say this is only history.

How many popular histories, encyclopædias, and school text-books have blindfolded Jesus by an apologetic paragraph on "the Carpenter of Nazareth" or "the Greatest Jew who ever lived," or "the Great Teacher of Galilee." These terms are utterly inadequate to the subject. Turn to the last edition of the Encyclopædia Britannica, and read the story of Napoleon or Charlemagne; and then turn to the utterly inadequate article about Jesus Christ. Turn to H. G. Wells' "History of the World," and read his paragraph on Jesus Christ, and you will see that H. G. Wells, with all his literary genius, deliberately blindfolds Jesus.

The same is true when unbelief blindfolds the Bible. You and I have done it by closing its covers, by preventing its message from reaching childhood, by omitting family prayers, by abandoning it on the shelf, and by making it, as Mark Twain once defined it, a "classic which every one talks about, but no one reads." You try to escape the living Christ by blindfolding Him in the only place where He can gaze at you, covering the Bible from the members of your own household.

Men blindfold Christ even in the pulpit, or in the Press, and then when they have blindfolded Him, it is so easy to mock His prophetic office and Messianic glory, and His claims to be very God of very God. Some preachers do not try to find out how great Jesus Christ is by studying the Gospels and the Epistles, but how small they can make Him. They tell you to omit Colossians and Revelation and Ephesians, where you have the effulgence of His glory. They read Mark's Gospel, but they do not turn over to the pages of John's Gospel because there they see too much of the brightness of His glory and the effulgence of His heavenly greatness. When men minimise Christ by any kind of critical process, instead of magnifying Him, they strike Him in the face.

Voltaire, Netzsche, Renan, Strauss, Paine, Ingersoll (and others like them in mind and heart, although not in notoriety outside the Church), and many who claim to be inside the Church, all agree together first to blindfold Jesus before they deny His Deity; to hide His face before they smite His glory. That kind of photophobia is often found in the homes of Christians, in our children when they come back from the University or High School.

Now what is *the cause of this tragic photophobia?* John says it is not mental, but moral; it is not of the mind, but of the heart. They hate the light, and they love the darkness " because their deeds are evil." The Greek word is *phaula*—poor, paltry, ugly, vulgar. According to our blessed

Saviour there is moral obliquity at the root of all refusal to accept Christ. This is perfectly obvious when you remember that Jesus is " the Light of the World." To refuse to accept the ideal which He presents is naturally to prefer darkness rather than light.

To draw closer to Him even gropingly, is to greet the Light, to hail the brightness of the morning. One of our most telling commentators on this Gospel passage, the German theologian, Lange, has this observation : " As on the trees of the same forest, all kinds of birds take shelter together during the night ; but in the morning, as soon as the sun shoots his rays thither, some close their eyes and seek the darkest retreat, while others shake their wings, and salute the sun with their songs ; so the appearing of Christ separates the lovers of the day from the lovers of the night, mingled till then in the mass of mankind." Where light is refused, photophobia sets in. Paul says : " If our Gospel be hid it is hid to them that are lost, in whom the god of this world hath blinded the minds of them which believe not, lest the light of the glorious Gospel of Christ, Who is the image of God, should shine into them."

If you are neglecting your morning watch, if you are omitting your daily Bible study, if you are forsaking the assembling together of the saints as the manner of some is, you may be sure that all of these things are early symptoms of photophobia, and will end in spiritual blindness.

On the other hand, if men draw near to the Light, God meets them. Erasmus wrote to Sir Thomas More about Plato, and said : " Where such light as exists has been conscientiously used, more is sought, and welcomed when it comes. Plato was like a man shut into a vault, running hither and thither, with his poor flickering taper, agonizing to get forth, and holding himself in readiness to make a spring forward the moment a door should open. But it never did. ' Not many wise are called.' Plato had climbed a hill in the dark, and stood calling to his companions below, ' Come on, come on, this way lies the East ; I am advised we shall see the sun rise anon.' But they never did. What a Christian Plato would have made ! " Those were the words of Erasmus to Sir Thomas More.

You and I who are living in the twentieth century, have only to read carefully the life of Gandhi, the most prominent figure in

India, and then to read the life of Chiang Kai-Shek, the most prominent figure in China, who, when he saw the gleam leapt toward it, and to realise the contrast. Chiang Kia-Shek bowed down before Jesus as his Saviour and Lord. But the lowest among the outcaste Christians is greater than Gandhi, because they have come to the light, while he has deliberately blindfolded Jesus although he follows Him afar off.

Finally, we have *the cure of photophobia*. We have it in the words of Jesus. " He that doeth the truth cometh to the light, that his works may be made manifest that they have been wrought in God." Christ is the panacea for all the ills of humanity. More light is the only cure for photophobia. " In Him is no darkness at all." " If we walk in the light as He is in the light, we have fellowship one with another, and the Blood of Jesus Christ cleanses us from all sin."

Dr. James Moffatt has a very fine translation of my text which I will read to you : " Anyone whose practices are corrupt loathes the light, and will not come out into it, in case his actions are exposed ; whereas, anyone whose life is true, comes out into the light to make it plain that his actions have been divinely prompted." Tell me, are you following the gleam, or are you trying to escape it by going back to the gloom ? Believe me, the principle of unbelief is not primarily intellectual, but moral.

When Jesus spoke to Nicodemus, it was night in Jerusalem. The city had a population of nearly a million people at Passover time—so Josephus tells us—in the days of our Lord. Jerusalem was a great city, with its outlying hamlets, and with all the evils of a great Oriental city. " Jerusalem which spiritually is called Sodom, where also our Lord was crucified." Many evil-doers were wandering abroad in the streets of the city, pursuing guilty aims that night. Many of them were victims of greed, or passion, or pride. But Nicodemus went through the main highway, and along a side street, and up a narrow staircase, and he came to Jesus by night. This groping after the Light was the promise of full enlightenment. It always is, as we missionaries on the foreign field know ; and our hearts leap with joy when some Nicodemus comes to us by night, saying : " Sir, we would see Jesus," whether it be a penitent publican or an irreproachable Pharisee. Those who seek find ; to those who knock, the door is opened. I love the words of Sankey's old hymn :

> "The whole world was lost in the darkness of sin—
> The Light of the World is Jesus.
> Like sunshine at noonday His glory shone in:
> The Light of the World is Jesus."

It was when men came seeking Jesus, when they drew near to the Light, that He revealed the greatness of His loving heart. Take two instances. One was when Christ was a Babe resting on the bosom of His mother Mary ; and the Wise Men came and opened their treasures. I cannot help but believe that when they looked into those eyes they saw in them Heaven's welcome for the whole Near Eastern world which to-day is coming nearer to Christ. Then we read in John's Gospel of those unknown Greeks, who said to Philip, " We would see Jesus." And you read further on in the chapter : " Now is the judgment of this world ; now shall the prince of this world be cast out "—the Greeks and all nations coming unto Him, the Light of the World. We see Mary Magdalene at the Feast, and Peter in the Hall, and the thief on the Cross, with all their sins, and all their shame, and all their denials, but they were sincere in their penitence, and they looked toward the Light.

Whenever I read the story of a penitent faith, I put in the margin this question : " How small a gospel can contain the whole Gospel ? " I think of him who looked simply to Jesus, the King of the Jews, conscious of his own sin, the first penitent sinner to enter Paradise. " This day shalt thou be with Me in Paradise." Jesus always gives forgiveness and peace and joy to anyone who comes to the Light. An English poet, Henry Vaughan, has put what I have tried to say of Nicodemus in unforgettable lines :

"Most blest believer he,
   Who in that land of darkness and blind eyes,
Thy long expected healing wings could see,
   When Thou didst rise;
And (what can never more be done)
Did at midnight speak with the Sun."

Nicodemus at midnight spoke with the Sun of Righteousness Who was there with healing in His wings—was there for Nicodemus. " To them that fear His Name shall the Sun of Righteousness arise with healing in His wings." Healing for all your hurts ; balm for all your woes ; comfort for all your griefs ; light for all your darkness. " He that doeth the truth cometh to the Light." "The path of the just shineth more and more unto the perfect day." "Awake thou that sleepest, and rise from the dead, and Christ shall give thee light." Cast off your photophobia. "And they shall see His face, and His Name shall be in their foreheads ; and there shall be no more night there, for the Lamb is the light thereof."

IV

The Glory of the Impossible

IV
The Glory of the Impossible

I RECALL that it has been my privilege to speak on three occasions here at Keswick on this subject of the Evangelisation of the Moslems. In 1907 I spoke on the will of God for the Mohammedan world. In 1915 I spoke of the fulness of time for the Moslem world. And most of us then thought that there was the dawning of a new day in Turkey, but it proved to be a false dawn. In 1923 I spoke on the patience of God in the evangelisation of Mohammedan lands from the text : " Master, we have toiled all the night and have taken nothing. Nevertheless, at Thy word I will let down the nets."

To-night our subject is the Glory of the Impossible in Moslem Evangelisation. That verse in Psalm 72 : " He shall have dominion also (or reign) from sea to sea, and from the river unto the ends of the earth," is one of the hardest passages in the Bible to believe. Unto men this is impossible, but with God all things are possible. For thirteen long centuries Mohammed—not Christ—has reigned from sea to sea across Arabia. The history of Missions in every land is the story of the achievement of the impossible. Yet this one promise taken literally means that Jesus Christ shall have dominion over all Arabia. This promise is repeated three times, in Exodus, in Zechariah, and in this Psalm.

For thirteen centuries we have waited for the fulfilment of this one promise. Arabia has been penetrated, it has been unveiled; but Arabia has not yet been evangelised. The story of Arabian exploration, which is the glory not only of Denmark and France and of the Netherlands, but especially of Britain, is known to every one. As Toyohiko Kagawa said : "If you are willing to die for it there is nothing you cannot accomplish." "Thou hast made Him a little lower than the angels ; Thou has crowned Him with glory and honour and put all things under His feet." In the story of exploration, men and women have been the incarnation of an attempt to do the impossible "in the strength which God supplies."

> "So near is grandeur to our dust,
>   So close is God to man,
> When Duty whispers low, 'Thou must,'
>   The youth replies, 'I can!'"

It is, however, not in the realms of science or exploration that I am speaking; for it is in another realm that we see the glory of the impossible—*in Christian Missions*. Eleven men standing on Mount Olivet, ignorant, unlearned, feeble in faith, faltering in trust—" when they saw Him they worshipped Him, but some doubted." And to them came the great commission, and in less than half a century they had accomplished the impossible, and covered the Roman Empire with the Name and the love and the power and the spirit of Jesus Christ. They remembered Christ's words : " All things are possible to him that believeth."

Now when we turn to the Mohammedan world and its evangelisation, we face a task that is humanly impossible and supremely difficult. I remember Gairdner, when he came to see me once in Cairo, struck the table in his earnest way, and said : " This is an impossible possible problem ! " Think of the colossal dimensions of what we call the Moslem world. Think of its ever-expanding area ; think of the building of mosques to-day in Paris, Berlin, and London. Think of the baffling fact that Islam is the only religion which has defeated

Christianity and eclipsed it. Buddhism and Hinduism have never done that; but Islam has utterly wiped out areas once Christian, and blotted out bishoprics and churches where once they sang the glory of the Triune God.

Think of the categorical denial by the Mohammedans in their books and creeds of all that makes Christianity Christian; of their arrogant defiance of Christ's messengers and disciples by closing and keeping closed doors that were once open, and these doors have been barred and bolted for thirteen long centuries. Christ was born in Bethlehem, and there, five times daily, they hear the Moslem prayer-call.

But where Mohammed was born in Mecca no Christian has ever yet proclaimed the Gospel. Travellers have gone in and out, but not one missionary has stood at the gates of Mecca to gain entrance and proclaim the Name of Christ. Think of the hopes deferred and the hearts made sick by massacres, martyrdoms, and deportations. Have you read the recent novel, " The Forty Days on Musa Dagh " ? There we have an epitome of what the Oriental Churches have gone through for centuries.

What are the actual dimensions of this

THE GLORY OF THE IMPOSSIBLE 81

problem ? Islam is not confined to the Mediterranean basin, nor to three Continents. It has crossed the seven seas, and invaded all five continents. The Moslem population of Africa is over fifty million ; of India, nearly eighty million ; of Java, forty million ; of Dhina, between eight and twelve million. It is found in every country in Asia with the exception, perhaps, of Korea. It extends to South America where there are 250,000 Mohammedans ; and there are three and a half million Moslems in south-east Europe. Under the American flag, in the Philippine Islands there were 587,000 Mohammedans. Its total is 250 millions of people bound together by one creed, by one type of culture, and by one great defiance of the work of Christian Missions.

This great system eclipsed Christianity in Central Asia and North Africa from the seventh until the fourteenth century. The story of this conquest has been recently told by a Cambridge scholar, Dr. Laurence E. Browne. Islam, he points out, is the only great religion that came after Christianity, and yet defeated and well-nigh destroyed it in Central Asia, in Arabia, Persia, Syria, Egypt, North Africa, and even in Palestine, the land of its birth. Churches by the hundreds, we might say by the thousands, became mosques; bishoprics became provinces that paid tribute. The new Arab civilisation wrote its Mohammedan palimpsest over the old Christian tradition. Mohammed's name was exalted above every other name.

Armenians, Nestorians, Syrians, Copts, and Berbers were persecuted century after century, and passed over to Islam until the remnant of the faithful became like Samson, with eyes blinded, grinding in the prison-house of the Philistines. That is the tragic history of the Oriental Churches. But there is always in that history of the Church the glory of the impossible—*the faithful remnant*.

Then, again, the impossibility of this problem appears when we ask what Islam really is. A compact system of anti-Christian theism; a threefold cord not easily broken; social ideals, political power, and religious convictions twisted together until only the power of God can untwist and unravel that which Lord Curzon called " not a State Church, but something far worse, a ' Church State'." In this religion is all the strength of the Arabian pagan

The Glory of the Impossible

pride of language and culture. In this religion is all the strength of Jewish fanaticism to win proselytes. In this religion is all the strength of universalism in its outlook and conquest borrowed from Christianity.

Think of the strength of its creed, so defiant, so penetrating; the very words sound like a battle-cry. No one who has ever heard them from a mosque in Cairo, or in Arabia, or on the borders of Afghanistan, can ever forget them. Think of the solidarity of its fellowship. I visited Beira, in Portuguese East Africa, in 1925; there boys were being taught, and were collecting their coppers to put into a box to pay for an aeroplane to be used by the Riffs of Morocco against the French in a holy war. You cannot parallel that in Buddhism, or Confucianism, or Hinduism. Think of the annual pilgrimage to Mecca. They meet every year in a barren valley, with scarcely a tent to cover them, and in a temperature of a hundred degrees in the shade; and they come from every part of the Moslem world. China sends pilgrims to Mecca, and every Chinese pilgrim spends between eight and nine hundred dollars for his journey.

It has meant not only the eclipse of the Churches, but of the Christ. His Incarnation, His Atonement, His Resurrection, His finality as Lord and Saviour, are contradicted by the Koran. Sir William Muir, the great British administrator, at the close of his four-volume Life of the Prophet, says in the last paragraph : " It is my conviction that the sword of Mohammed and the Koran are the most fatal enemies of civilisation, liberty, and truth, which the world has yet known." And Islamic propaganda has not ceased ; it has entered the West. The Ahmediyya sect have built mosques in Berlin, London, and Chicago, and they are circulating new lives of Mohammed in English, Turkish, Albanian, Polish, Italian, Javanese, Malay, Dutch, Chinese, Hindi, Bengali, Tamil, and other languages. In their publications catalogue they claim to have published seven million pages of this literature in the last few years.

Not only is this religion defiant of Christianity in its creed and propaganda, but down at the centre of it is the old law of apostasy, which is still in force in many lands, and which has made visible results meagre ; the battle for the truth is a fight against the wall. One of the saint-

THE GLORY OF THE IMPOSSIBLE 85

liest of British missionaries, Miss Lilias Trotter, of North Africa, wrote just before her death in Algeria ; " We who are engaged in Moslem work live in a land of blighted promises. That is a fact that none of us who love its people best can deny ; and the deadly heart-sickness of hope deferred, sometimes makes even the most optimistic of us almost despair of seeing abiding fruitage to the work." She was not a pessimist. A pessimist is a man who blows out the candle to see how dark it is. She was living in the light of God ; she was feeding on the promises of God, with the light of Christ in her very soul. She faced reality. And we need once again to face the glory of this impossible task. And as God did years ago, so now again He will raise up men and women who will go forth to this great conflict, conscious that they have the strength of God and the power of God with them.

Look at the actual situation. I do not say that there are no results. I have seen the work of God's Spirit among the Mohammedans in Java. I have seen the public baptism of twenty-two adult Mohammedans in St. Luke's Church, Isfahan. I have seen Mohammedans in Arabia who had surrendered all for Christ, and who faced life with nothing, no friends, no home, no hope—their one hope was in Christ Who had died for them.

Yet look at the actual situation. Think of the thin red line, Christ's vanguard, His lonely sentinels. Egypt has had eighty years of unremitting sacrificial toil by the noblest of men and women of the Presbyterian Mission and the Church Missionary Society, and yet there are scarcely three hundred Moslems converts in all Egypt to-day, from Alexandria to Khartoum. In Arabia forty years of pioneer effort against prejudice, and loneliness, and a deadly climate—hospitals, schools, evangelism, toil and tears and blood—and all the visible results are a little handful of Christians! And yet not one of them would change places with any one of you; they are holding on in the glory of the impossible.

Missionary work in Turkey is far more difficult than it was twenty-five years ago. North Africa, which once boasted Athanasius, Augustine, Cyprian, Tertullian, thousands of churches and scores of bishoprics, now counts scarcely more than a little group of small organised Christian Churches.

There is not a missionary to-day in all

THE GLORY OF THE IMPOSSIBLE 87

Tripoli to keep lonely vigil; and none in all western Arabia; and three little stations in all Central Asia; with a few waiting wistfully on the borders of Afghanistan, while some have penetrated and returned. Yet none of them would exchange places with us because they are confident of the issue. They see the invisible, they lay hold of the intangible, they hear the inaudible voices. There is no great ingathering, but they know that the promises of God are sure, and they know that He shall yet have dominion from sea to sea. With men this problem of Islam seems impossible, but not with God.

The Roman Catholic Church published a striking book recently. I read it with great interest. It was entitled, " *The Psychology of Conversion.*" These learned missionaries and—whatever else we may say of them—devoted missionaries, had chapters on the psychology of all the non-Christian religions, and the approach of the Gospel message. I turned to the last chapter, it was entitled, " *Le bloc inconvertisable —les Musulmans*!" Thank God, the Protestants have never used that word in regard to the Mohammedan world! They have never lost faith in God since the day of

Raymund Lull, and Henry Martin, and Canon Gairdner, and the other heroes of the Cross. Bible circulation is our Protestant glory. Like dynamite that Word of God has been used to blast the rock of Islam to pieces.

We hear of the veil disappearing in Turkey, and being forbidden in Persia, and of the rights of womanhood being recognised. All this is another illustration of the power of God's Word. Doors once barred and bolted are now opening. Ibn Saood has repeatedly invited medical missionaries to visit his capital. Missionaries have crossed over into Afghanistan, and preached the Gospel to the Mullahs of Herat. That is the glory of the impossible.

We say Afghanistan is closed, and from within comes this voice. Let me read to you what an educated Afghan says in a book, " *Lights of Asia,*" in which he writes on Christianity and other religions. He says : " Christianity centres in the Cross. The Cross is the centre of all revelation. Have you ever thought what the Bible would be without the Cross ? Take the Cross out of this Book, and you will not be able to recognise it. The Old Testament without the Cross is lost. Put the Cross back, and at

The Glory of the Impossible

once the Book becomes a Gospel. Christians find the Cross the centre of their religion. In sorrow they sing : ' Simply to Thy Cross I cling.' When they pass through the valley of the shadow of death they sing : ' Hold Thou Thy Cross before my closing eyes.' The Cross is the place of victory. If I want my sin conquered, if I want to get it beneath my feet, I must find Christ first upon the Cross. I say it reverently, Christ Himself could not do it but for the Cross. It was expedient for one Man to die for the people. He has put away sin by the sacrifice of Himself. ' He only could unlock the gates of Heaven and let us in.' Social reform could not do it ; ethical sermons could not do it. Only Christ on the Cross can forgive and conquer sin in the human heart." All this in a chapter on Christianity by an Afghan Mohammedan !

We see those closed doors. Do we realise that the Bible penetrates, that literature penetrates, that God's Spirit penetrates ? To-day we see across the great Mohammedan world great darkness. But the pent-up energies of unanswered prayer ; the prayers of His saints now before His throne ; the faith of those who saw the invisible before they fell asleep ; the visions of the noble army of martyrs, from Raymund Lull, and Henry Martin, and William Borden—all these are creative forces which God is now using to accomplish the impossible. It is daybreak, not sunset in the Moslem world. The mosque of Santa Sophia no longer hears Muezzin's cry; it has become the museum of the new Turkish Government, and every one who passes through it sees in those glorious mosaics, where the plaster has been removed, the story of the Gospel, the baptism of Jesus, the Crucifixion of Jesus, and the Resurrection of Jesus, portrayed in marble by the early Christians, and now made visible by a secular government. Those who visit the old mosque at Damascus can see these words inscribed: " Thy Kingdom is an everlasting Kingdom, and Thy dominion from generation to generation." There is only one thing that is impossible—it is impossible for God to lie. His promises are sure.

> "Uplifted are the gates of brass,
> The bars of iron yield,
> To let the King of glory pass.
> The Cross is in the field."

That Cross has never been defeated, because it itself was the defeat of sin, and death, and hell. He Who hung on it will

The Glory of the Impossible

yet have dominion from sea to sea, and from the river unto the ends of the earth. If you want a task worthy of your powers, if you want a real apostolic succession, I appeal to you to put your life on the altar for this most difficult of all missionary problems, and to have the patience of the saints, and the faith of the martyrs, and the endurance of those who see the invisible.

V

The Hinterland of the Soul

V

The Hinterland of the Soul

I WANT to show how hard it is for you and me, for a Salvation Army officer, or a Bishop of the Church of England, or a narrow, proud Presbyterian, to be freed from all those things that bind us, and to enter into the boundless heritage of Christianity.

This challenge of King Ahab: " Know ye that Ramoth-gilead is ours, and we be still, and take it not out of the hand of the king of Syria ? " (1 Kings 22. 3), and the words of Paul the Apostle : " All things are yours, whethe. Paul, or Apollos, or Cephas, or the world, or life, or death, or things present, or things to come ; all are yours " (1 Cor. 3. 21, 22), have nothing whatever in common, except that both of these men were imperial in their thinking. Ahab thought of his hinterland on the borders of Gad, overrun by the enemies of Israel. His statement was perfectly true. Ramoth-gilead was included in the promise of God to Abraham, in the division of the land by

Moses, and in the establishment of this city of refuge. Although Ahab was killed in battle, his son Joram captured Ramoth, and the Jews to-day on the front page of the newspapers, are claiming that very city as their own.

Paul thought of the spiritual heritage of those who were in Christ Jesus, of their boundless possessions as Christian imperialists; and he said that all Christian teachers, with all their gifts and talents, of the world of Paul's day, of the whole Roman Empire, of things present and things to come, of death itself—they were the possession of the Christian.

This hinterland of the soul is the little-known, untravelled land of spiritual experience; it is the vast and undeveloped territory which Christ has gained for us by His death and resurrection, and which is our common spiritual heritage. Like the hinterlands in the history of imperialism, they await pioneers and empire builders to pour their hidden wealth down to the coast.

You remember the story of European imperialism in its four chapters, at least our youth remembers it—of discovery, exploration, exploitation, and possession—

the British, when they took Aden in 1837, and later Singapore; the French at Algiers in 1830; the Dutch at Capetown; Cecil Rhodes dreaming his dreams at Johannesburg. And Mussolini planting the Italian flag on the hills at Addis Ababa. Now such conquests and such exploitations are mostly morally indefensible. But Paul summons us here to spiritual imperialism, and neither he, nor the Christian hymn-book which we use are ashamed of using a military vocabulary.

Of all the forms of Pacifism, Spiritual Pacifism is the most despicable. "For we wrestle not against flesh and blood, but against the rulers of the darkness of this world, against the principalities and powers" that conspire to keep us out of our God-given heritage, the possession which Christ has won for us on Calvary. Therefore we must fight if we would reign.

> "Increase my courage, Lord.
>   I'll bear the toil, endure the pain,
>   Supported by Thy Word."

Just two questions. What is the hinterland of the soul? What is the area, what are the boundaries of our spiritual possessions? And the second question: Does it really all belong to you? The boundaries

Paul gives us in a long inventory; and after giving the inventory, Paul gives us the title-deeds to our vast inheritance, namely, "Ye are Christ's, and Christ is God's." "All these are yours, because ye are Christ's, and Christ is God's." Now, leaving out the title-deeds, let us take a survey of our possessions.

The sovereignty of God the Father is the corner-stone of all property rights in the universe; the redemption in Jesus Christ confers on those who have received the adoption, the glory of their inheritance. They sing:

> "My Father is rich in houses and lands,
> He holds all the wealth of the world in His hands;
> Of jewels and diamonds, of silver and gold,
> His coffers are full; He has riches untold."

I am the child of a King. Alas, most of us have never realised our possessions! Most of us live on the narrow coast, and we have never ventured inland; we are afraid, we are timid, we are sectional, we are parochial, we are sectarian souls, poverty-stricken, emaciated weaklings. One says, "I am a Presbyterian;" another, "I am a Calvinist;" another, "I am a Methodist;" another, "I am a Fundamentalist;" an-

The Hinterland of the Soul 99

other, "I am a Low Church Anglican;" another, "I belong to the Salvation Army;" another, "I am a Friend." Now, none of those who use those phrases in an exclusive sense have ever realised the greatness of their inheritance.

We forget that the smaller the hinterland the smaller our resources. The smaller the diameter of your brother-love, the smaller the circumference of your spiritual power. But, as the Psalmist says, we shall "run the way of God's commandments when He shall have enlarged our hearts." Just think of that phrase, and what it means; you can meditate on it, and it gets bigger and bigger as you think of it. "All are yours."

Paul, the Roman citizen, educated at Tarsus, learned in all the learning of the Jewish Talmud, with an imperial outlook. Apollos, a Greek, Hellenist, Alexandrian. Peter, a Jew of the Jews, a fisherman who spent three years in the greatest Theological Seminary ever founded, on the shores of the Lake of Galilee, sleeping with the Master in the boat, who was with Him face to face through those years. All these are yours.

Now the impression we receive of a man's spiritual wealth or poverty depends entirely upon the area which he keeps cultivated in the garden of his soul. Only Christ can give magnanimity and largeness of heart. Only Christ is the inexhaustible fountain of tolerance, love, and sympathy. Only Christ can endow us with our common inheritance in the holy Catholic Church of which He alone is the Head.

Again and again we meet in every walk of life, and in our friendly circles, men and women who have no better coast-lines than we have, and yet who seem to have far greater reserves, and larger horizons, and much ampler resources of power. If you have shaken hands with Moody, as I have, and if you have looked into his eyes, you know you have seen a man of spiritual resources. The same was true of Charles Spurgeon, or to speak of living men, John R. Mott and Robert E. Speer. There is a largeness and a wideness of horizon about their spiritual life that become the envy of those of us who are following afar off.

When we seek the reason for this great wealth of personality, we find it to be none other than this: These men and women have obeyed the remarkable words of Obadiah and " possessed their possessions." (You can easily find the words, because

THE HINTERLAND OF THE SOUL 101

there is only one chapter in Obadiah.)

These men and women have brought unoccupied territory into cultivation. They have sunk hidden shafts, and found new lodes of wealth. Perchance Dr. Jowett gave them the vocabulary of pure spiritual English. Dr. Alexander Whyte taught them the exceeding sinfulness of sin. Bishop Phillips Brooks led them to a new discovery of the sheer beauty of holiness. Toyohika Kagawa was their teacher in the school of sacrifice for Christ. And Bishop Lancelot Andrewes taught them how to pray.

To possess your possessions does not depend on circumstances or natural talent; it depends on your will. " Whosoever *will* may enter in." John Bunyan had no advantages, except that he was arrested and put in jail; and when he was in Bedford Jail he travelled all the way to the Celestial City, and gave us a guide-book, than which there is none better. Luther in the Wartburg translated the Bible into such household German that he led captive a whole nation to the feet of Jesus Christ. Such heroic souls not only explore new territory, but they write the guide-books for other pilgrims to the City of God.

All of you know that common word

"Baedeker." A German scholar first thought of writing guide-books for all countries and places; and there was a time when there were no better guide-books than the Baedekers. What a shelf we have of these Baedekers of the soul! Bishop Andrewes' great book of "*Private Devotion*" has no equal in the realm of prayer. Thomas à Kempis on "*The Imitation of Christ*" has no equal to make us home-sick for Heaven. John Cordelier, the great Roman Catholic mystic, wrote a little handbook, "*The Pathway of Wisdom*," which I would not myself like to lose from my library. Charles Gordon's "*Letters to his Sisters*," when he was engaged in a campaign of blood and fire in Khartoum, is one of the strongest books of devotion you can read. Arthur's "*Tongue of Fire*" still stirs a fever in the blood of age. Forbes Robinson's "*Letters to his Friends*," to which someone introduced me, opens extraordinary new vistas of other-worldliness, and the patience of the saints. And then there is that priceless little book—to be had for sixpence anywhere—"*The Practice of the Presence of God*," by Brother Lawrence. He was a scullion in a monastery. With those books on our book-shelves, and taking time to wait on God, what a saint you could be, if you could master even these seven little Baedekers of the soul.

Or turn to our hymn-books. All our great hymns are the result of spiritual adventures, the bold ascent, the mountain-top experience, the ascent up Everest of men like Heber, Faber, Wesley, Newman, Isaac Watts, and George Matheson, or women like Frances Ridley Havergal, who found their way to the City of God, and left a record of their mountaineering. hymn-book to believe once again in the One needs only to study the pages of the Holy Catholic Church. The Presbyterian hymn-book has a very old hymn by Andrew of Crete, and it is my favourite hymn :

> "Christian, dost thou see them
>   On the holy ground?"

It is one of the greatest hymns dealing with temptation. Some of these hymns stir our souls because they mount upwards into the hinterland.

You say : "I have often read these books." Yes, and you have done exactly what the impecunious world-traveller does; the trick of the American stay-at-home, who sends to Europe and secures hotel labels, and pastes them on a suitcase that has never left New York harbour! It is not enough to possess your Baedeker. The only way to follow these saints of God is to go into the highlands yourself, to explore its secrets, to unearth its treasures, to dare to leave the coast. Because all things are yours when you cross the old frontiers and press beyond your parochial barriers.

How suggestive is the thought of the Apostle that each of us may supplement our own narrow lives, and enrich them by possessing the immortal parts of every great and noble life that has ever lived! Even the mere contemplation of the great moments of the past produce enlargement of the soul.

One has only to compare the mental outlook of the reader of one local daily newspaper with that of the man who can sit down any day he chooses in a great library, and hold communion with the intellectual life of all the ages. As Emerson says:

> "I am the owner of the spheres,
> Of the seven stars and the solar years,
> Of Cæsar's hand, and Plato's brain,
> Of Lord Christ's heart, and Shakespeare's strain."

Now, according to Paul, not only the

great characters of the past, but the future itself is ours too. All things are yours. " The world to come." What did he mean ? Although in one sense the future belongs to everybody ; in another sense it belongs only to those who are in Jesus Christ. In the first century the future belonged, not to the men who thought that Paul was a fool, but to Paul the Apostle.

In the thirteenth century the future belonged not to those powerful bishops and Popes who did their utmost to restrain and silence St. Francis of Assisi and Raymund Lull, but to them.

In the sixteenth century the future belonged to Martin Luther and John Calvin, it did not belong to His Holiness the Pope.

In the eighteenth century the future belonged to John Wesley ; it did not belong to those influential ecclesiastics who crowded him out of their churches and forced him, against his own inclinations, to preach in the open fields. Now to whom does the future of the twentieth century belong save to those Christians who are already looking beyond the horizon, who can read the signs of the times, and who makes bold adventures for God ?

That brings us to our second question.

To whom does all this vast hinterland belong? To whom else than to you? "All things are *yours*." "Jesus Christ the same yesterday, to-day, and for ever." His promises, His power, His presence, His Spirit. As Neander well says: "The sovereignty over the world was indeed conferred on man in his original estate. But this being lost through sin, was restored again by redemption. ('Ye are Christ's, and Christ is God's.') The spirit which is bestowed on Christians carries in itself a principle which everything must eventually obey, and which will subjugate the world ever more and more, until at last the promise, that 'the meek shall inherit the earth' is fulfilled, and the world has become the theatre of the divine kingdom." Until He shall reign from sea to sea, from the river unto the ends of the earth—until every knee shall bow, of things in Heaven, and on earth, and under the earth, and every tongue shall confess that Jesus Christ is Lord to the glory of God the Father.

"All things are yours." What does it mean? All true Christian teachers of every name—Paul and Apollos and Cephas and Wesley and Phillips Brooks and Cardinal Newman and Barth and Brunner and Pascal and Papini and Spurgeon and William Booth—we do not belong to them; no, they belong to us. Every faithful minister profits the whole Church; and every member of the Church may, and ought to, derive benefit from the teachings of all. It is thus our minds are expanded beyond mere party limits and party cries into a true catholicity.

> "For the love of God is broader
> Than the measure of man's mind.
> And the heart of the Eternal
> Is most wonderfully kind."

At the great Conferences at Oxford and Edinburgh, attempts were made to weld and bind together all those who love the Lord Jesus Christ so that no longer will it be ridiculous, but literally true when we sing :

> "We are not divided; all one body we. . . .
> "Like a mighty army, moves the Church of God."

The declaration " All is yours " also promises the world to Christians, pre-eminently in this sense, that all secular art and all the sciences help to furnish mortar for building the temple of God. Christians are not called to leave the world, or to curse the world, or to ignore the world, but to overcome the world, and to rule the world for God. Music, painting, sculpture, architecture, all the fine arts, they were given by God from the beginning of the creation to be used for the glory of God.

Any of you who have ever read the history of music, or painting, or sculpture, or architecture, will say, as a great artist said to me : " Every one of the fine arts have laid their finest tributes at the feet of Jesus Christ." The world is only a scaffolding that will be broken up when it has served its end in assisting to construct God's temple and throne for Jesus Christ.

I saw a letter from the Bishop of Natal (Bishop Hamilton Baynes) many years ago, when I was in South Africa. He wrote these words: " I am ready to hope and believe that a Church which has an imperial outlook, a world-wide plan, and a sure hope of peace among the nations of the world, may awaken a response among the people of England which can never be evoked by a merely personal and parochial religion which expresses itself in soup-kitchens and tracts." Soup-kitchens and tracts are good things, but surely we need to have a larger horizon of the power of the Church and of Christ its head.

Christ's promise is our Magna Charta,

our title deed. " I am come that ye might have life, and that ye might have it more abundantly." The Christian life has four dimensions—length, breadth, height, and depth. Like the love of God, it takes " all the saints " to measure it. For the Son of Man is Lord of all. Remember Peter's challenge to near-sighted Christians. He himself suffered at first from parochialism and narrowness of heart until he had the threefold vision on the housetop at Joppa, and then his heart was enlarged, and he felt the growing-pains of his soul, when he shook hands with Cornelius, and bridged the chasm between the two races, the Jew and the Gentile. Afterwards he wrote to the poor near-sighted Christians : " Add to your faith, virtue; and to virtue, knowledge; and to knowledge, self-control; and to self-control, patience; and to patience, godliness; and to godliness, kindness; and to kindness, love."

All this means a big-souled enterprise, an heroic effort; it means the conquest of the unoccupied hinterland. It means the appropriation of its riches and resources. Ahab said : " Why do we sit still ? " You are to be your own Livingstone. You are to be your own Cecil Rhodes. You are to be your own spiritual empire builders. For " all things are yours." Listen to Edwin Markham's trumpet call :

> "Are you sheltered, curled up, and content
>   By the world's warm fire?
>   Then I say, that your soul is in danger!
>   The sons of the light, they are down with
>   God in the mire,
>   God in the manger.
>   So rouse from your perilous ease;
>   To your sword and your shield;
>   Your ease is the ease of the cattle.
>   Hark! Hark! where bugles are calling
>   Out to some battle!"

Why do we sit still ? Why are so many people in our Churches content with a smug self-satisfaction. " Come, Holy Spirit, Heavenly Dove! " " Dear Lord, and shall we ever live, at this poor dying rate ? " " Ramoth-gilead is ours." The whole Land of Promise is ours. All things are yours. Claim them now. All the depth of the riches of love in Jesus Christ!

May God give you here at Keswick, and give me, largeness of heart in all our ecclesiastical borders. Let us go up and possess the land. For the path of eternal wisdom in all creation is growth by sacrifice and service. Let this Keswick Convention date the commencement of your expedition, the great adventure with God. Forward, march! Put on the whole armour of God—girdle, helmet, breastplate, shield, sandals, sword. Then close ranks, every one who loves the Lord Jesus Christ, and possess the land; "for all things are yours, and ye are Christ's, *and Christ is God's.*"

www.ingramcontent.com/pod-product-compliance
Lightning Source LLC
Chambersburg PA
CBHW071144090426
42736CB00012B/2213